William Wallace

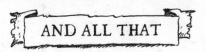

AND ALL THAT

William Wallace

AND ALL THAT

Allan Burnett

Illustrated by Scoular Anderson

BIRLINN

First published in 2006 by
Birlinn Limited
West Newington House
10 Newington Road
Edinburgh
EH9 1QS

www.birlinn.co.uk

ISBN 10: 1 84158 498 3
ISBN 13: 978 1 84158 498 0

British Library Cataloguing-in-Publication Data
A catalogue record for this book is available from the British Library

Designed by James Hutcheson
Typeset by Iolaire Typesetting, Newtonmore
Printed and bound by Cox & Wyman Ltd, Reading

For my wife Linda, the true heroine of this
and many other books

Contents

Sheriff William Heselrig awoke with a jump as his bedroom door was suddenly kicked open. There, towering over him, stood giant Scotsman William Wallace.

Before Heselrig could move a muscle, Wallace brought down his sword on the sheriff's brow and sliced his brain in half like a grapefruit. Talk about a splitting headache!

In a single stroke, by killing Sheriff Heselrig, Wallace became Scotland's wildest outlaw. An outlaw was someone who lived outside the law, hunted and feared by those in power – and celebrated by poor people everywhere. Before long, Wallace was the greatest outlaw in history . . .

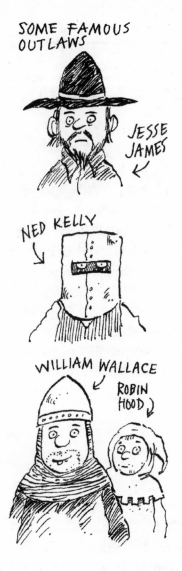

SOME FAMOUS OUTLAWS

JESSE JAMES ←

NED KELLY ↓

WILLIAM WALLACE ← ROBIN HOOD ↓

But hang on a minute. Was Wallace really the greatest outlaw ever? Greater than the famous highway robber, Robin Hood, who stole from the rich to give to the poor?

Much greater. Robin Hood was probably not a real person, he was just a made-up character. Wallace also stole from the rich to help the poor, yet he was definitely REAL – as real as you and me.

Surely Wallace couldn't have been as fearsome an outlaw as the great Wild West cowboy Jesse James?

Actually, Wallace was much more fearsome. Wallace killed his enemies without using pistols – just a sword, or even his bare hands.

What about gunslinging Australian bushranger Ned Kelly? He was an outlaw who stole from the rich and powerful to feed his poor family. Was Wallace really greater than him?

You bet. Wallace wasn't just a robber or a bandit, and he didn't just look after his own – he was a freedom fighter who became the leader of a whole nation.

You see, the sheriff that Wallace killed, Heselrig, was an Englishman. There's nothing wrong with that, of course – except that in Wallace's day, the Scots and the English were not the good friends they are now. In fact, they hated each other's guts!

The English had just invaded Wallace's home country of Scotland and stolen the Scots' land. The Scots had had their freedom taken away and were being treated like slaves. And the job of English sheriffs like Heselrig was to make sure the Scots couldn't do anything about it.

By killing Heselrig, Wallace showed he was determined to stop at nothing until he got his land back. After that, he would never rest until all Scots were free again. And he was willing to wage war against the mightiest army in Europe, the English army, to win his struggle.

As if all that were not reason enough for Wallace to get his hands dirty, there's also something else. According to reports, Heselrig had just murdered Wallace's beloved wife.

Heartbroken, Wallace wanted revenge – a dish that's best served cold. So after Wallace killed the sheriff, he chopped up the body up into meaty chunks. Ugh!

Make no mistake, Wallace lived in very bloodthirsty and savage times. And when people like Wallace wanted to settle their differences with somebody, they didn't tell their teacher or call the police. They splattered them!

Besides the fact that he splattered the sheriff, a lot of Wallace's early life is very murky and difficult to trace. In fact, nobody really knows for sure exactly how or when his adventures began.

The trouble is, there are many different stories about Wallace's rise to fame. Some of them are true, but some of them might not be. So first we have to learn how to tell the difference between Wallace facts and Wallace nonsense . . .

1

A hero with many faces

Have you ever heard about things being lost in the mists of time? Well, Wallace's life is a bit like that. Since Scotland is a very misty place, and Wallace lived a very long time ago, lots of facts about his life have gone missing.

After Wallace died, storytellers tried to look after the facts about Wallace's life in the same way that a museum looks after precious artefacts, such as swords or helmets. But museum artefacts can sometimes roll under a cupboard or get lost down the back of shelves. Likewise, bits of Wallace's story were sometimes lost by storytellers.

This happened often, because many bits of Wallace's story weren't actually written down at first. Instead, as the years passed, young storytellers had to learn about Wallace by listening to older storytellers. Remembering all the bits of the story wasn't easy, so many parts were soon forgotten or got muddled up.

To make up for the bits they forgot, storytellers added up new things to add to Wallace's story. This process of bits getting lost and new stuff being added turned Wallace's life story into a legend. A legend is half true and half fantasy.

Around the year 1470, many years after Wallace died, a harp-playing storyteller called Blind Harry the Minstrel finally had all of Wallace's adventures written down in a book. By then, Wallace's legend had grown very large indeed. So Blind Harry's book is a mixture of truth and nonsense, or facts and fantasy.

It's usually not too hard to tell which bits of Blind Harry's book are nonsense. We know that some bits are false because other, more reliable, books about Scotland in Wallace's day contain a different version of events. Other bits of Blind Harry's book seem just too outrageous to be true.

For example, Blind Harry tells us that Wallace once had a fight with a hungry lion in a foreign land – and survived. It might be true that Wallace really did fight a lion, but then again it might not. If it was true, the chances are Wallace would have ended up as cat food!

Another suspicious side to Blind Harry's story is that it's very repetitive. It goes a bit like this:

Well, after the battle, Wallace won another battle – then he won two more battles – then Wallace decided to fight a battle...

In Blind Harry's story, Wallace never had time to stop for a chat about the weather or to do the washing-up, because he was always fighting somebody! Blind Harry just loved to harp on about Wallace's endless victories in battle.

Many of these battle stories have to be taken with a pinch of salt. The fact is that no real man, not even a hero like Wallace, would have had the time or the strength to win as many battles as Blind Harry claims he did.

But when Blind Harry's book about Wallace first appeared, most people believed what they read. The book became very, very popular. So popular, in fact, that many hundreds of years later, bits of Blind Harry's story were used to make a Hollywood movie about Wallace called *Braveheart*. Like Blind Harry's Wallace, the film *Braveheart* is an exciting mixture of facts and fantasy.

The book you are reading now contains a lot of facts about Wallace's life, as well as many traditional Wallace stories and legends that include bits which may or may not be true. If you use your common sense, though, you can judge for yourself whether a story is *likely* to be true.

Figuring out the truth about Wallace's life is a bit like trying to work out what he really looked like. Take all the statues, paintings and other versions of Wallace that have been made over the years, for example. We have:

Angry Wallace - this version of Wallace was built in 1814 at Dryburgh, in the Scottish Borders. See how Wallace scowls across the border at England with his big, wide eyes.

Hunky Wallace – this version of
the hero on the Wallace Monument
at Stirling was made by the Victorians
during the mid nineteenth century.

Hairy Wallace – this Wallace has
a great big bushy beard. You can
find beardy Wallaces in Paisley
Abbey and in the Scottish National
Portrait Gallery in Edinburgh.

Tanned Wallace – Australian actor
Mel Gibson played the part of Wallace
in the film *Braveheart* in 1995 and now
there's a statue of Mr Gibson as Wallace
at Stirling.

Fancy–Dress Wallace – the great hero
is so popular today that people dress
up and pretend to be him. They also
pretend to fight his battles again for
fun, with their friends dressed up as
enemy soldiers.

So Wallace is a hero with many faces, but which one is the right one? Nobody really knows, but he probably had a beard or moustache of some description.

We definitely do know that Wallace was a big man. Come to think of it, he was almost a whopping seven feet tall. That's more than two metres!

According to one report written not long after Wallace died, he was: 'A tall man, with the body of a giant. Cheerful in appearance with agreeable features, broad-shouldered and big-boned, with belly in proportion and lengthy thighs.' So definitely a bit of a hunk, then.

In fact, we know that Wallace must have been good-looking because he had lots of girlfriends. On the other hand, there are lots of basic facts about Wallace that we are still not sure about.

For example, we don't even know for certain how old Wallace was. He could have been born any time between the years 1260 and 1280! But the clues suggest his birthday was probably some time around 1272.

Then there's the question of where he was born. Nearly everyone agrees that Wallace was born somewhere in the south-west of the country, but the tricky question is where *exactly*?

Some people think Wallace popped into the world in Elderslie, which is near Paisley in Renfrewshire. They say his dad was called Malcolm Wallace of Elderslie.

But other people believe Wallace is the victim of a dreadful spelling mistake, and he was really born in the village of Ellerslie in Ayrshire. And some say that Wallace's dad wasn't Malcolm at all, but was actually Alan Wallace of Ayrshire.

WHERE HUNKY WALLACE MIGHT HAVE BEEN BORN.

SCOTLAND

ELDERSLIE
ELLERSLIE

As for Wallace's mum, she was called Joan. Or Jean. Or perhaps Margaret. Nobody knows for sure who she was, never mind where she gave birth to Wallace.

Those who reckon Wallace came from the village of Ellerslie, or somewhere nearby, point out that he definitely spent lots of time in Ayrshire when he was young.

For example, it is said that Wallace got into furious arguments at a place called the 'Bickering Bush' in Ayrshire. Perhaps the bush was one plant that didn't like being talked to?

We know for a fact that Wallace also had a hideout or 'den' in Ayrshire, which is where he was living when he hacked up Heselrig.

It's no surprise that Wallace needed a hideout, because by the time he got into really serious trouble it seems he was already known across the country as a bit of a brigand, or petty thief.

The English rulers of the city of Perth certainly had their eye on him. In 1296, they made note of 'a thief, one William le Waleys'. Waleys was an old spelling for Wallace.

If Wallace was a known thief, that might explain one legend about his early brushes with the English authorities. The story goes that Wallace was wandering through his local market in Ayrshire one day, carrying a few fish he had caught in a nearby river. He was just minding his own business when two soldiers appeared:

But Wallace didn't believe the Scots needed permission from the English to do anything. It was the English who had stolen the Scots' land and waters in the first place, thought Wallace, along with all the animals and fish in them.

So how did Wallace react when he was accused of being a thief? Perhaps he said:

Not Wallace – it's quite clear that this humble young country gentleman was no pushover. So maybe he said:

But the tall and muscular Wallace was probably in no mood for bargaining, either. In fact, if Wallace said anything at all it was more like 'Here's the sharp end of my sword – take that, you rats!'

Two skewered soldiers later, Wallace's reputation as an outlaw started to grow.

Wallace was clearly a clever fellow and he had probably done well at school when he was a lad. It is said that young Wallace went to the Grammar School of Dundee, on the east coast of Scotland, and lived in a nearby village called Kilspindie.

According to another story, schoolboy Wallace got into trouble with the English authorities in Dundee, too. Apparently, the son of the English governor of Wallace's town was a bully, who always picked on Wallace and his family.

One day, Wallace decided enough was enough and tore into the toerag with his sword. Again, we can't be sure whether this story is true or not – but it sounds like Wallace, all right!

When he wasn't getting into trouble after school, Wallace was also educated by two wise uncles who were priests in the Church – a very powerful organisation in

those days. Wallace's uncles taught him some very important lessons.

The first lesson Wallace learned was how to read and write in Latin, which was a language used all over Europe for very important business.

The second lesson was how to read and write in French, also a language used for very important matters. Wallace would be able to use French and Latin to call on powerful people across Europe to help him when he got into really deep trouble – but more about that later.

Of course, Wallace also knew the native languages of Scotland. These were Gaelic, which was spoken all over the country in those days, and Inglis, which later became known as Scots.

As well as preparing his mind for the adventures that lay ahead, Wallace had to exercise his body. One way of doing this was hunting.

In the great forests that then covered Scotland, Wallace learned how to ride horses expertly and hunt for wild animals like tusked boar – while avoiding the jaws of deadly wolves.

Another way to get in shape was to become a warrior. Wallace learned how to fight enemy warriors with weapons like axes, swords, spears, dirks, daggers and long-bows with arrows. (Though probably not all at the same time!)

To protect himself, Wallace wore armour hidden under his clothes – so that strangers wouldn't know his real fighting strength. His outfit included the following fashion-able items:

BASCINET
(LIGHT STEEL
HELMET)

HABERGEON
(CHAIN MAIL
HEAD AND
SHOULDERS
PROTECTION)

TOUGH
GLOVES

TUNIC
(THICK, LONG
CLOTH SHIRT)

GOWN
(PROTECTION
FROM BAD
WEATHER
—AND GOOD
DISGUISE)

All of this meant that Wallace was well prepared for fighting the English when the time came. Before we begin Wallace's adventures properly, though, there is one big question that needs answered.

How did Wallace's country end up under English rule in the first place?

Two royal knockouts

Scotland's problems began in 1286, when Wallace was probably still a teenager. It was all King Alexander III's fault.

Alexander was a good king, wise and strong, who had ruled Scotland peacefully for almost forty years. But nobody's perfect, and Alexander was no exception.

One night, while he was at a feast in Edinburgh Castle, Alexander decided he wanted to go and visit his young French wife, Yolande, for a bit of romance. Nothing wrong with that, you might say.

Except on the night in question, it was blowing a ferocious gale and Queen Yolande was forty miles away in the royal palace of Kinghorn, Fife.

To get to his wife, Alexander had to follow bad, narrow roads, and take a ferry across the treacherous waters of the Firth of Forth. Then the king had to ride along the cliff tops above the Fife shoreline with waves crashing below and the wind howling all around.

The ferryman begged him to turn back, but Alexander wouldn't listen. He had guzzled lots of wine before he left Edinburgh Castle, making him very stubborn and tipsy.

So Alexander galloped off into the murk, along the windswept cliff tops. But instead of concentrating on controlling his horse on its treacherous journey, it seems the king thought of little else except hugs and kisses with the lovely Yolande.

So what do we think happened next? Surprise, surprise, Alexander's horse lost its footing in the darkness and high winds, and the king was sent sailing through the air to meet his doom. He landed on the beach with a royal thud, breaking his neck, and that was the end of him.

So Alexander was one of those kings who really did meet his downfall. Or you might even say he was a jilted lover.

Anyway, the king's death was bad news for Scotland because he didn't leave behind a son to take over from him. People in those days thought kings made stronger rulers than queens, so the Scots weren't very happy when they realised that Alexander's only heir was his granddaughter Margaret, the Maid of Norway.

Margaret was just a little girl, and the Scots were worried that having her as queen would make the country easy for invaders to attack. It would also make it more likely that the Scots would quarrel among themselves.

So somebody hit on the bright idea of asking King Edward 'the Longshanks' next door in England to come and help decide what to do next. England was a rich and powerful kingdom, with at least three times as many people in it as Scotland. That made Longshanks one of the most respected kings in Europe, so it seemed to make sense to ask him for advice.

The Scots didn't realise yet that Longshanks was actually a scheming villain, who wanted to build an English empire to rule over Scotland and make the Scots his slaves. But they would soon find out.

Longshanks, who was nicknamed Longshanks because of his long legs ('shank' is an old word for the bit of leg between your knee and your foot), at first pretended to be nice and helpful. He suggested marrying little Margaret to his eldest son, Prince Edward, to keep relations between the two countries friendly. Of course, the English king kept secret his real plan, which was to use the marriage to seize control of Scotland and make it a part of England.

But before she could be lured into Longshanks' trap, poor wee Margaret was struck by tragedy in 1290, while she was being taken across the North Sea from Norway to Scotland. Even though Margaret's boat crossed the water safely, the voyage was very long and conditions on her ship were very bad by today's standards. She became seriously ill and didn't survive the journey.

To lose one monarch may be regarded as a misfortune. But to lose two seems like carelessness. In the space of four short years, Alexander had bitten the dust – okay, sand – and Margaret had died before she could blow out the candles on her eighth birthday cake.

What would the Scots do now?

3

Longshanks the villain

The Scots hadn't a clue what to do, so they turned again to Longshanks. This was a disaster, especially for you and me because it makes the next bit of the story quite complicated.

Trouble was, the Scots now had no direct heir to the throne. Instead, loads of people began claiming the throne was theirs – but only one could become king. So the Scots needed Longshanks to help decide who should be crowned before a huge row erupted. Longshanks agreed to judge a competition for the crown, provided England was allowed to look after Scotland's affairs until the winner was picked.

No sooner had the Scots agreed to this than the penny began to drop with them that Longshanks was up to no good. Before the competition was over, he started tightening his grip on Scotland. He demanded that castles were handed over to English control and pushed Scots out of important jobs, replacing them with his cronies from England. The Scots protested but Longshanks insisted all this was for their own good.

However, when a kind of English police force took control of Scotland, they soon started rubbing locals up the wrong way. Arguments broke out. Then scuffles. Then riots.

Now, I know what you're thinking: this is where Wallace comes crashing back into the story. Well, almost. His dad got into a fight with the English at a place called Loudoun Hill in Ayrshire.

According to one report, Wallace's dad had his legs almost cut off by an English knight called Fenwick. But Wallace senior refused to give in, and carried on fighting on his knees. Wallace's dad probably had a few other bits chopped off him before he finally said to Fenwick and his followers something like 'Okay, you win. But I'll get you next time!'

Unfortunately, Wallace's dad never got the chance – the story goes that he was skewered to death there and then by English spears. Young Wallace must have been devastated when he discovered what had happened . . . and very, very angry.

After a while, the riots across Scotland calmed down a bit and some kind of peace was restored. For now.

Eventually, in 1292, Longshanks picked a winner in the

competition for the crown – a nobleman called John Balliol. But Balliol barely had time to try the crown on for size before Longshanks began bossing him about and treating the Scots as his slaves.

The last straw came when Longshanks demanded that the Scots follow him into a war against France. The Scots had no quarrel with the French, and saw no good reason for starting a fight with them. So they refused.

When Longshanks found out, he went berserk. In 1296, he gathered his army in Newcastle, near the English border with Scotland, and prepared for an invasion.

In response, every Scotsman was ordered to take up arms to defend the kingdom. Scotland was about to begin its War of Independence!

4

Scotland gets squashed

For a while, the Scots and English eyed each other, waiting for someone to make the first move. The trouble started when Robert de Ros, an Englishman living near the border, apparently decided he wanted to marry a Scottish lass.

It could have been a match made in Heaven – but de Ros' family didn't see it that way. As far as they were concerned, de Ros had turned against his own folk and sided with the enemy. Worse still, he planned to let the Scots use his castle as a base to attack the English.

De Ros' relatives were having none of it. They asked Longshanks to send some soldiers north with orders to turn the black sheep of their family into mutton.

Unfortunately for the English soldiers, the Scots saw them coming – just like lambs to the slaughter. Longshanks' henchmen were ambushed and killed.

So did this nasty little episode make the two sides realise that violence was not the way to settle things?

Of course it didn't. By now, everybody was itching for a fight. So Longshanks unleashed his bloodthirsty troops on the border town of Berwick.

Berwick was a very important Scottish seaport, over-flowing with riches. It was where ships loaded with cargo sailed to and from ports across the North Sea, making it a lifeline between Scotland and the rest of Europe. Until, that is, Longshanks' army turned up.

By the time the English were finished there, Berwick was just a ghost town. Around twenty thousand Scots had been slaughtered, and Scotland's lifeline to Europe was cut off.

Once all of the Scots bodies were dumped in the sea or thrown in huge pits, Edward immediately began rebuilding Berwick.

Then Longshanks rolled his army north to Dunbar. But the Scots had been roused into action by Longshanks' barbarity in Berwick, and were ready to put up a fight.

A Scottish army turned up at Dunbar Castle, where the

garrison were under siege by the English. The Scots in the castle reckoned the tables were about to be turned against their attackers and began jeering at them.

When people wanted to be nasty to the English in those days, it was common to joke that they had tails. So the Scots began waving their banners and shouting at their foes: 'Tailed dogs, we will cut your tails off!'

But the English had the last laugh, after they outwitted and then splattered the approaching Scottish army. You can imagine what the Scots inside the castle might have said now: 'Er, we were only joking about the tails. Please don't kill us!' Fat chance.

What the Scots needed now was a king who was smart and strong enough to snatch victory from the jaws of defeat. Unfortunately, Balliol wasn't that kind of king.

Instead, Balliol chickened out and surrendered in July 1296. He was hauled before Longshanks at Montrose, south of Aberdeen, and forced to resign as monarch.

Longshanks grabbed Balliol and ripped the Scottish king's royal crest from his jacket, or tabard, throwing it to the floor.

After that, Balliol was nicknamed Toom Tabard, which meant 'empty jacket' or, in other words, 'king nobody'. He was thrown into an English jail, although he was later allowed to go and live in France.

In the meantime, Scotland was kingless (again). To show that he was now in charge, Longshanks went to Perth and stole the Stone of Scone. The Scots were horrified.

But what was so important about a stone, which to those not in the know sounds like something you spread butter and jam on? Well, here are some clues:

ROCK-HARD FACTS AND CRUMBLY MYTHS ABOUT THE STONE OF SCONE

1 What is it made from? To some people it might sound like a cake that's been left in the oven too long, but the Stone of Scone was made of rock.
2 Why is it important? Since the beginning of history, Scottish rulers sat on the stone during a special coronation ceremony to become king. (Try sitting on a fruit scone and you'll realise why the stone had to be made of real rock!)
3 Why is it called the Stone of Scone? It's named after a place near Perth called Scone, where the coronation ceremonies took place. Of course, the correct way to say Scone isn't the same as the cake you have with tea. Instead, stick your lips out in an 'Oooh' shape and say 'Scooooon!'
4 Does it have any other names? It is also known as the Stone of Destiny.

5 Why did Longshanks want it? He wanted it in order to show he was the ultimate ruler of Scotland, and to make sure nobody else could become King of Scots without his permission.

6 So where did he take it? Longshanks took the stone to Westminster and hid it under his throne, where it was stored for seven hundred years until it was officially returned to Scotland in 1996. It is now in Edinburgh Castle.

7 What is it worth? If it's the *real* Stone of Scone, it's priceless. But it might actually be a fake! Some people believe Longshanks was tricked, and the lump of yellow sandstone rock he stole wasn't really the Stone of Destiny.

8 So what did Longshanks steal, then? Apparently, he was given the stone lid of the toilet used by monks at Scone Abbey and assured it was the genuine article.

9 Does that means the real Stone of Scone is still waiting to be discovered? Perhaps. Some people believe the real stone is made of marble and was originally used as a (not very comfy) pillow.

Whether Longshanks stole the real Stone of Scone, or just the lid of the monks' toilet, he certainly made a stink in Scotland.

When the English king returned to his headquarters at Berwick, he set up a new English government to rule over Scotland. He ordered all Scots to swear loyalty to him and pay their taxes to England.

Scottish landowners were made to sign a document called the Ragman Roll, promising that they would do as they were told from now on – or be outlawed. And if an outlaw was caught, they usually became a dead outlaw.

The Scots were now well and truly English slaves. The English controlled their land, their money and their freedom. All Scots had to obey English orders at all times. But can you guess who refused to do as he was told?

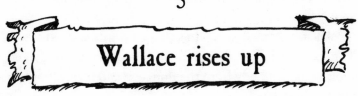

5

Wallace rises up

As we have discovered, Wallace probably had loads of reasons for hating Longshanks and the English rulers of Scotland by now. So there was no way Wallace was going to be an English slave. Instead, he hit back.

Many other Scots wanted to do the same. So when they began hearing stories about the giant rebel William Wallace and his exploits, they started joining him. According to one report, Wallace learned of a strong but arrogant English soldier in the town of Ayr who would let you hit him across the back with a pole if you paid him a groat (four pence, but worth a lot more in those days).

So Wallace gave the soldier three groats, then whacked him with the pole so hard he broke the soldier's back.

When the soldier's friends tried to punish Wallace, he broke the neck of one and smashed another over the head with a heavy club called a cudgel. Then he took out his sword.

Wallace sliced up another two soldiers before jumping on his horse and galloping off to the woods where he couldn't be found.

In a story about another bloody brawl with some English

soldiers in Ayr, Wallace wasn't so lucky. He was captured and carried off to a dungeon, where his enemies left him to starve.

Wallace became very ill and slipped into a deep sleep. The English believed that their prisoner was dead, and took Wallace's body from the dungeon and threw it onto a smelly dung heap.

Wallace would have died for sure, except his friends heard about what happened and secretly took his body away. While they were cleaning all the muck off Wallace, they noticed his eyelids flickering and realised he wasn't dead after all.

Wallace's survival was seen as a miracle, a bit like the resurrection of Jesus in the Bible. A famous old wise man called Thomas the Rhymer heard about Wallace's miraculous recovery and predicted that Wallace would lead the Scots to freedom.

Thomas the Rhymer was famous because people believed he had magical powers, which allowed him to see into the future. The old man had correctly predicted the death of Alexander III before it happened, so the Scots were sure he was also right about Wallace.

When Wallace got better, it is said he wanted to make sure the friends who had rescued him were not put in any more danger. So he left them behind and set out for Glasgow, armed only with a rusty blade.

Once Wallace was on the road, the story goes that he wore a disguise so nobody would recognise him. But he was met by an English officer and his two guards on highway patrol, who stopped him in his tracks. That was their first mistake.

The Englishmen were wary of the disguised man. They thought he looked suspiciously like that big outlaw they had all been hearing about called Wallace, and wanted to take him back to Ayr. That was their second (and last) mistake.

He says he's just a poor old beggar.

Wallace pulled out his rough weapon in an instant. He sawed through the officer's throat, hacked off the head of one guard and then chased after the other – grabbing him and then ripping his stomach open so his guts spilled out all over the place. Yuck! Yuck! Yuck!

The blood-soaked Wallace then helped himself to the dead men's armour and horses – as well as their silver, which he would need to buy food and other supplies.

After that, it seems there was no let-up of Wallace's killing spree, so be warned: the next few pages are splattered with more blood and guts. Ugh!

6

Bloody revenge

Remember Fenwick, the knight who killed Wallace's dad? So did Wallace. According to one story, Wallace found out that Fenwick and a large troop of English soldiers were escorting a treasure chest filled with Scottish silver and gold through Ayrshire.

So Wallace decided to take his revenge by ambushing Fenwick at Loudoun Hill – the very place where the English knight had reportedly killed his father.

Helped by a growing band of loyal followers, Wallace pounced on Fenwick and his men. Fenwick tried to skewer Wallace with his lance, but Wallace jumped out of the way and then sliced through the straps attaching Fenwick's saddle to his horse.

The English knight toppled to the ground, and was stabbed to death by one of Wallace's companions. With their leader Fenwick finished off, those English knights and foot-soldiers that hadn't been killed already fled away in panic.

When news of Wallace's success spread across the country, the Scots were impressed. Wallace proved that a small band of Scots could take on a much larger force of heavily armoured English knights and men-at-arms – and win. According to reports, he shared out his loot among his followers, and people began to think of him as a real-life Robin Hood. Or rather a very, very bloodthirsty Robin Hood.

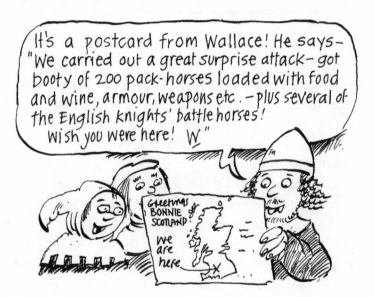

As Wallace's fame grew, the reports of his adventures became more and more gruesome. After all, he lived in barbaric times, especially since Scotland and England were not the good neighbours they are now.

Of course, if anyone behaved like that today they would be punished and locked up in prison forever. But because of the times he lived in, it's pretty clear that Wallace had no choice but to deal with his problems the old-fashioned way – he hacked, slashed and sliced his way through them.

All of Wallace's hacking, slashing and slicing made the English desperate to catch him. So it was important for Wallace to have lots of hiding places.

The forests that ran thick all around Lanarkshire, Ayrshire and the Borders had endless nooks and crannies that Wallace and his men squeezed into. And there were caves, too, where nobody could find Wallace in the darkness.

Most of the forests are long gone today, although if you go to places like Selkirk Forest, which still has thick patches of woodland, you can imagine Wallace and his merry men creeping through the undergrowth on their way to whack one of their enemies. And there are other hideouts that you can still visit, like Wallace's Cave near Coalburn in Lanarkshire.

Striking out from these secret places, Wallace and his band of outlaws scored a string of victories against much larger English forces, at places like Shortwood and Queensberry. He also drove the English out of many important castles.

But Wallace was still an outlaw, and not yet a commander who could lead a proper Scottish army against the English. Then something appears to have happened to change all that. Wallace fell in love . . .

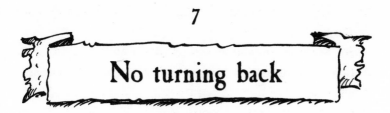

7

No turning back

After having a few girlfriends, it seems that Wallace decided to settle down and marry a girl called Mirren Braidfute. We are told that the couple had a daughter, some time in the Spring of 1297.

Young Wallace apparently fell in love with Mirren after he first clapped eyes on her near the town of Lanark, at St Kentigern's Church, which is today a romantic ruin. It seems that Mirren felt the same way about Wallace and soon began helping him by letting his men hide out in her house.

The trouble was, Wallace apparently wasn't the only man who fancied Mirren. The story goes that the fearsome English sheriff of Lanark wanted to marry her to his son. (Parents were always interfering in their children's lives, even in Wallace's day.)

By the way, the name of the sheriff should sound familiar from the start of our story . . . William Heselrig. Heselrig must have been hopping mad when he found out that Mirren had married Wallace, who in his view was a gangster and rebel.

A chance for Heselrig to have his revenge soon arrived.

According to the story, Wallace and his men were crossing the street in Lanark when some English soldiers began insulting them.

Soon, the two sides came to blows and swords were drawn. The street battle that followed was a gruesome affair.

According to further reports, Wallace chopped the hand off one of his enemies and blood spurted from the soldier's arm like a ketchup bottle that's been squeezed too hard!

The gore splattered all over Wallace's face and blinded him for a moment, but not long enough for the other English soldiers to get the better of Wallace and his men.

The Wallace gang fought their way back to Mirren's house, ran right through it, and then escaped through the back door. From there, they sprinted off and disappeared into a nearby rocky chasm called the Cartland Crags.

Wallace was sure Mirren would be safe if she kept her front door locked and acted innocent when Heselrig and his men came knocking. But Heselrig was suspicious of anyone friendly with Wallace, especially Mirren.

The sheriff ordered Mirren's front door to be broken down. She was seized by English soldiers, her house was burnt to the ground and the young beauty was murdered on the spot.

There is no gravestone or death certificate to prove that Mirren was killed by Heselrig. But if the story of her death is true, then we know that by May 1297 two of Wallace's nearest and dearest – his dad (probably) and his wife – had been killed in cold blood by the English authorities.

One thing we are sure of is what Wallace did next: he killed Heselrig. In fact, he didn't just kill him; Wallace slaughtered the sheriff with such violence that it sent shivers down the spine of every English soldier in the land.

According to the report revealed at the beginning of our story, Wallace went straight round to Heselrig's house, kicked the door in and ran upstairs to find the sheriff in his bedroom. In an instant, the giant outlaw swung his sword down with such force that it split Heselrig's skull in two, right down to his collarbone.

Since Heselrig had been one of the most powerful of Scotland's English rulers, Wallace realised that there was now no turning back. Once Longshanks found out what had happened, he would stop at nothing to ensure Wallace was wiped out.

But that was easier said than done.

8

Helping hands

By killing Heselrig, Wallace suddenly became much stronger, because he made the Scots realise that the mighty English could definitely be beaten.

Once, Wallace had had only a small band of men, but now an army began flocking to his side. It even included some soldiers and knights who decided to leave the English army, because they admired Wallace for standing up to Longshanks.

To help make his army strong enough to drive out Longshanks' forces once and for all, Wallace turned to the help of some powerful Scots:

When Wishart joined Wallace it angered the pope, who was Wishart's boss and world leader of the Church. The pope was very pally with Longshanks, but that didn't frighten Wishart. Instead, Wishart encouraged Wallace to join forces with another Scottish rebel called:

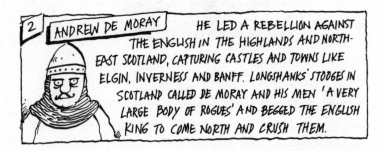

ANDREW DE MORAY HE LED A REBELLION AGAINST THE ENGLISH IN THE HIGHLANDS AND NORTH-EAST SCOTLAND, CAPTURING CASTLES AND TOWNS LIKE ELGIN, INVERNESS AND BANFF. LONGSHANKS' STOOGES IN SCOTLAND CALLED DE MORAY AND HIS MEN 'A VERY LARGE BODY OF ROGUES' AND BEGGED THE ENGLISH KING TO COME NORTH AND CRUSH THEM.

If it wasn't for Wallace and friends like de Moray, England would have conquered Scotland by now. Most of the Scots nobles were too busy bickering among themselves over who should be king now that Balliol had been booted off the throne.

After causing a bit of trouble for Longshanks, these rich nobles were told that none of them would be king and all their lands would be taken away forever if they didn't behave.

Many of the nobles owned land in England as well as Scotland, so they didn't want to upset Longshanks too much. In July 1297, they again promised to do as they were told from now on.

Over the next few years, the Scottish nobles would bend this way and then that way – sometimes supporting Wallace, sometimes supporting Longshanks. And always thinking about what was best for themselves!

Meanwhile, Wallace's warriors and de Moray's men-at-arms continued harassing the English wherever they went. Splitting up into groups of highwaymen and assassins, they robbed English convoys and splattered any English officials they could get their hands on.

With their growing army, Wallace and de Moray soon took control of all of Scotland north of the River Forth. The town of Dundee tried to keep them out, but they slowly began crumbling it like Dundee cake. Then they set their sights on the great fortress of Stirling Castle.

When Longshanks heard about this, he decided that enough was enough. He ordered a giant English army of 30,000 soldiers to march north and lay waste to Wallace's warriors and de Moray's men-at-arms. The real battle for Scotland was about to begin . . .

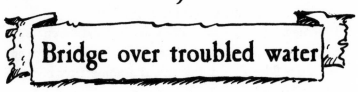

9

Bridge over troubled water

The English and Scottish armies met a few miles north-east of Stirling Castle on 11 September 1297, on either side of the River Forth. Led by the Earl of Surrey, the English marched up to the southern banks of the river, while Wallace and de Moray's men came down to arrive at the northern banks.

Historians disagree with each other about what exactly happened next, but it went something like this. Wallace and de Moray got to the river first, with about 10,000 men. Then the Scots watched as the English army gathered on the banks opposite them. The English army was the most experienced and battle-hardened in all of Europe – and was three times bigger than the Scottish army.

But the Scots on Wallace's side hadn't come all this way just to turn back now. Sure their leader Wallace and his sidekick de Moray were young. Sure they had never taken on an army this big before. And sure they faced almost certain death . . .

But, hey, at least they were rebels with a cause. They would rather die as free Scots than live as English slaves.

Besides, Wallace had a plan. According to some reports,

he put his men up on top of a big rocky hill called Abbey Craig, which guarded a shallow ford where the English could otherwise have crossed the river easily.

This meant the English had to think of a different way to get across. There was another place further upstream called the Kildean Ford, but it was a non-starter because it was so far away.

At least that's what the man who held the purse strings in Surrey's army said. He was the treasurer, a plump and arrogant chap called Hugh Cressingham.

It will cost too much money to take the army up to Kildean ford...

...and it will be a waste of money to take the army home again – let's just get on with it!

Surely the best way to 'get on with it' was to just swim across? Well, you try swimming across a river when you're dressed up in heavy armour and weighed down with lots of metal weapons. On second thoughts, don't try that unless you're a fish.

Seriously, the quickest way for the English to get on with it was a narrow wooden bridge standing right in front of them. This was known as Stirling Bridge.

According to the maps the English carried with them, Stirling Bridge was indeed the swiftest way to get from the southern half of Scotland to the northern half without getting your feet wet.

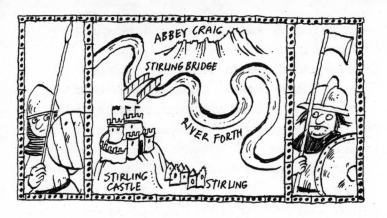

So it must have been glaringly obvious that all the English had to do was go straight across the bridge, right? Not to Surrey. He was afraid of the bridge for two very good reasons:

REASON 1 BRIDGE TOO NARROW. KNIGHTS COULD ONLY CROSS TWO AT A TIME.

REASON 2 GROUND ON OTHER SIDE OF BRIDGE TOO BOGGY. ENGLISH KNIGHTS HEAVY HORSES WOULD GET STUCK IN THE MARSHY GROUND.

GLOOP

Eventually, Surrey reluctantly agreed to cross the bridge. He hoped that Wallace would wait too long before coming down off the hill to attack, because then there would be enough English cavalry and foot-soldiers across the bridge to smash the Scots.

Except Wallace was too smart to make that mistake. He expected Surrey's force would have to start crossing the bridge sooner or later, which they eventually did.

Things were going just as Wallace had planned. Now he waited until only as many English as the Scots could handle got over the bridge to his side. Then he sprung his trap . . .

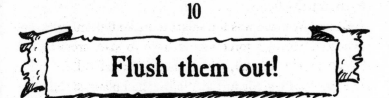

10

Flush them out!

Spearmen rushed down at Wallace's command to attack the English, getting in behind the enemy so they couldn't retreat back across the bridge. Then Wallace sent in his main force of swordsmen to attack the enemy head on, skewering their horses and making haggis of their riders as they fell to the ground.

Wallace and de Moray led from the front as the blood and guts of hundreds of English foot-soldiers were splattered all over the place. At one moment during the fighting, de Moray was badly wounded by the enemy – but Wallace kept on fighting as the Scots became stronger and stronger.

'On them! On them! On them!' cried the Scots. 'Off us! Off us! Off us!' the English probably replied – but the Scots weren't listening.

Chased by the Scots, some panic-stricken English knights and men tried to escape back across the bridge. But this just sent them crashing into new English forces coming the other way!

Soon the the narrow bridge became jammed. There was nowhere left to go but over the side. So men and horses jumped, fell or got pushed off the bridge and splashed into the waters below. The English had fallen into Wallace's trap – and now they were being flushed out like a blockage from a toilet.

On the south bank of the river, Surrey and the rest of the English force could see their chums either being clobbered or swept into the river by the small Scottish army. They began to worry that the Scots might be supermen who would swim over and slaughter them all.

Realising that all was lost, Surrey gave the command to retreat. He ordered the bridge to be set on fire to try to keep the Scots at bay – even though that meant leaving the last of his men on the north bank to their doom.

Surrey galloped away from the field with such haste that his poor horse didn't eat until he got back to England. But Cressingham wasn't so lucky.

According to reports, Cressingham was so big and heavy

that when he tried to turn his horse around, he rolled off his saddle and tumbled onto the ground. He huffed and puffed, but couldn't get back up again.

Then one of Wallace's warriors ran at him with a big Lochaber axe. Cressingham shouted out in French for mercy, but unfortunately that particular Scot didn't understand French. So he chopped Cressingham's block off.

According to further reports, things then got even more gruesome. Since Cressingham had been a big chap, Wallace and his men decided to make use of his fleshy body. They used his skin to make belts, scabbards, saddles – you name it. These were grisly souvenirs of the Scots' victory at the Battle of Stirling Bridge, as it became known.

The Battle of Stirling Bridge was certainly savage, but what a victory! It paved the way for Wallace and his men to take control of Stirling Castle and send the English packing. Scotland had won her freedom at last!

11

Freedom

So Wallace won freedom for his people at Stirling Bridge. But what exactly is freedom, anyway? Freedom is being able to do whatever you want, with whoever you want, whenever you want to. Within reason, of course.

Nowadays, apart from having to do the washing-up and tidy our rooms, or go to school or jobs, we are all pretty free. We take freedom for granted. But for Wallace to get his freedom, he had to break the yoke of slavery.

The yoke of slavery is when somebody else bullies you, treats you like dirt and makes you do whatever they say all the time. A 'yoke' is also a word for a wooden frame that's put over a person's shoulders so they can be made to work hard all day long, without a rest, carrying heavy buckets of water for somebody else. You can see the similarity, can't you?

The yoke of slavery is not to be confused with the yolk of slavery, which is when somebody forces you to eat the yellow runny bit of an egg even though, behind your polite smile, you don't really want to!

THE YOKE OF SLAVERY

THE SLAVERY YOLK

With victory over Longshanks' army at Stirling Bridge, Wallace well and truly smashed the yoke of slavery. Now the English couldn't tell the Scots what to do.

So does that mean the Scots lived happily ever after, then? What do you think!

12

Back in business

Longshanks had thought it would all be so simple:

When he found out that Wallace had won the Battle of Stirling Bridge, Longshanks hit the roof. Spluttering with rage, the king of England vowed to forget France and return to Scotland himself as soon as possible with an EVEN LARGER army to grind the Scots into porridge oats.

When he got his hands on the upstart Wallace, Longshanks planned to tear him limb from limb.

In the meantime, though, Wallace was basking in glory.

He and de Moray sent letters to people all over Europe, telling them that the Scots had beaten the English and were free again.

One of their letters was taken to a place in Germany called Lübeck by two Scottish merchants called John Burnet and John Frere. It went something like this:

Dear citizens of Lübeck,

Since your town is the most important place for trade in the whole of northern Europe, we thought it important to let you know that Scotland is open for business as usual.

No doubt you heard about the spot of bother we had, what with the English taking away our land and our freedom and killing anybody who tried to stop them. But that's all ancient history now.

So please don't be put off trading with us. Your merchants will be perfectly safe if they come here – honest.

Yours sincerely,

Andrew de Moray and William Wallace, leaders of Scotland's army

This letter and others like it showed that Wallace and de Moray didn't just want to win battles, they wanted to make life better for the Scots.

If you remember, Longshanks had cut Scotland's lifeline to Europe by seizing the port of Berwick and killing all the Scots traders there – the Lübeck letter was designed to fix that lifeline by starting up Scottish trade again. Trade with Europe meant the Scottish people could buy things that they needed, and sell things to earn more money.

Then Wallace had a bit of bad news. The ink was barely dry on the Lübeck letter before poor de Moray died from the wounds he had suffered at the Battle of Stirling Bridge. So Wallace was left to lead the Scottish army on his own.

Wallace decided to attack the north of England, as a warning to the English not to get any ideas about invading Scotland again. The locals in places like Northumberland and Cumbria were terrified. 'The Scots are coming!' they shouted as they ran from their fields and villages in panic.

Wallace's raids on England were horrendous, and lots of people were killed. Many Scots reckoned they deserved revenge after being made to suffer under English rule. But it was probably not a good move, because it encouraged English reporters working for Longshanks to make up stories that pretended the Scottish raids were even worse than they really were.

Wallace was certainly no saint, but these reports were mostly lies to blacken Wallace's name. Nevertheless, many folk believed them. The English people urged Longshanks to get back up to Scotland and whack Wallace as soon as possible.

Longshanks was more than happy to oblige. He was already preparing his army to march north by the summer of 1298.

Back in Scotland, Wallace was prepared for the next battle that lay ahead when he was knighted as Sir William Wallace and made Guardian of Scotland. This meant Wallace wasn't just the leader of Scotland's army any more – he was the leader of the country, like a prime minister or president today. Since there was no king to speak of apart from old Balliol, who was just a lame duck hiding in France, Wallace was now the most powerful man in Scotland.

Or at least he should have been.

Unfortunately, Wallace's promotion made a lot of other important Scots jealous. Even though Wallace had freed Scotland from Longshanks, some Scottish nobles still thought he was just an upstart.

But why? Well, most nobles believed that you could only be a leader of a country if you were rich and owned lots of land. The trouble was, Wallace wasn't rich, and, according to some reports, he personally didn't own very much land at all. Even though Wallace was not a poor peasant, many nobles thought of him as one. They didn't think he deserved to be Scotland's leader.

By the time Longshanks' army started marching north for another showdown, many of these grumbling Scots nobles decided they wouldn't support Wallace. In fact, some of them even decided to fight for Longshanks instead.

While Wallace reportedly stopped by the little village of Riggend to sharpen his sword on a boulder he must have cursed those wretched nobles. He was on his way to Falkirk to meet Longshanks' army. Things were about to turn really nasty.

13

Time for another battle

It was a misty morning outside the town of Falkirk on 22 July 1298 when Wallace spied Longshanks' army preparing for battle. Reports say that Wallace stood on a big rock on top of a hill, so that he could get a better view of the English army as the sound of its war drums got louder and louder.

Wallace knew which direction Longshanks was coming from, but unfortunately we don't. The exact spot where the Scots and the English clashed for the Battle of Falkirk is a mystery. Some say it was to the north of Falkirk. Some say it was to the south. Others say the east and, you guessed it, there are those who reckoned it was to the west. Just thinking about it is enough to make you dizzy.

Wallace must have been dizzy too when he saw the size of Longshanks' army. After the humiliation of Stirling Bridge, the English king had decided this time that he would come up personally to Scotland to sort Wallace out, with the largest army he could muster. One report claims there were a whopping 87,000 men in it.

So what exactly does an army of 87,000 men look like? Well, imagine watching a very wide procession of angry people marching towards you, with its tail stretching off into the distance as far as the eye can see.

Hmm... don't tell the lads but I think we might be outnumbered.

There were many hundreds of armoured knights on great big battle horses called destriers. The knights held brightly coloured shields and flags. There were lots of other cavalry with banners and loud horns. And there were thousands of foot-soldiers and archers – all armed to the teeth.

Then there were loads of followers, such as blacksmiths and cooks, baggage carriers and mule drivers. They were all ready to pitch in, too, if they were needed. In fact, Longshanks' army might have been so big that if it were around today it would fill any of the biggest football stadiums in the world.

Some historians claim the size of Longshanks' army was nearer to 15,000 men – but it was still a lot larger than Wallace's. Wallace only had about 8,000 in his army, possibly far fewer. For Wallace and his men, taking on Longshanks' horde was like one football team trying to play against at least two others at the same time – and still win.

To try to make it a more level playing field, Wallace and

his men had already gone around southern Scotland leaving nothing but scorched earth for the advancing English. This meant that houses, fields and crops were all burned – and animals taken away.

As a result, Longshanks' army couldn't find any food for themselves or their horses. According to one English report, all that they came across was one skinny cow – definitely not enough to feed an army of thousands!

Enjoy it – It's your dinner and breakfast!

Things got so desperate that Longshanks ordered some ships to sail up the coast from England to Scotland bringing food and supplies for his men. Except that when the ships did turn up they were, according to reports, loaded mostly with wine. Longshanks decided to let his men drink it, which was a mistake. With hardly any food in their bellies they got drunk and began brawling among themselves.

The English were tired, hungry, bruised and fuzzy when they reached the spot where Wallace was waiting for them. But that probably made them all the more determined to splatter the Scots so they could go home and have a decent meal and a good rest.

To help make light work of the Scots, the English army had lots of wagons and trailers carrying big scary weapons. These included:

1. **Gunpowder** - this was used to make a smoke bomb called Greek fire, which exploded over the enemy with a flash.

2. **Siege engines** - these included giant catapults called trebuchets, which launched rotting animals and boulders at the enemy, as well as battering rams.

3. Mobile bridges and ladders – no way was Longshanks going to let his army get caught out again by rivers, bogs and marshes. So he brought everything he needed to cross water or climb banks and walls, just in case.

Meanwhile, Wallace had brought a secret weapon of his own. He had been breeding a special kind of giant 'hedgehog' called a schiltrom (or schiltron). A schiltrom wasn't a real hedgehog, but a very large squad of soldiers holding long spears.

When the spearmen all stood together in a tight group, with their spears facing outwards, they looked like a giant hedgehog. If an English rider galloped into the schiltrom to attack, his horse would be skewered and so would he – so the schiltrom was a very sturdy weapon.

But Wallace needed more than giant hedgehogs if he was to win this battle. Unfortunately, all Wallace had was words. As the English prepared to begin their attack, Wallace roared at his men:

I have brought you to the ring, now you must dance as best you can!

Aw, I wish he'd told us sooner – I've brought the wrong shoes!

But this was no time for *dancing*. It was a time for fighting! What was Wallace on about?

In fact, when Wallace said 'dance' what he really meant was fight – but maybe some Scots got confused and actually started dancing. That would certainly explain why things started badly for the Scots and then got worse.

14

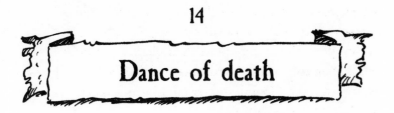

Dance of death

Battle commenced when the English cavalry surged forward like two big waves. The first wave of riders spilled into a bog that had been cunningly disguised by Wallace and his men.

But the second wave made it through and crashed ferociously against the Scottish schiltroms.

Wallace's men were immediately in trouble, but the schiltrom hedgehogs held firm and at first the English couldn't break through. Many of Longshanks' cavalry were skewered with schiltrom spears and ended up looking like giant horse-shaped lollipops. The riders landed on the wet, marshy ground with a loud squelch – and then got clobbered.

Things might have started going Wallace's way, except that Longshanks had a particularly nasty surprise in store – his archers.

The English archers used a fancy longbow that could hit a target much further away than the Scots archers, with their puny bows and arrows, ever could. The English archers didn't need to be anywhere near the schiltroms to start picking off the Scots spearmen one by one.

Gradually the schiltrom hedgehogs got weaker and weaker. This allowed more and more English riders to come forward, swinging their swords and lopping off Scottish heads. Now the going got really tough. Wallace needed all his men on foot and on horseback to stand firm if they were to have any chance of success.

But at the crucial moment, some of the Scottish nobles who had bothered to turn up for Wallace began to slink away to save their own skins. Without a proper cavalry of nobles, Wallace's army was doomed.

On the other side of the field, Longshanks stood and watched the Scots nobles turn and disappear into the trees. The English king could see that things were going his way, and must have felt very pleased with himself. Maybe Longshanks' horse felt sorry for Wallace though, because during the night before it had kicked the English king in the chest and cracked a couple of his ribs.

But Longshanks was so full of poisonous hatred for Wallace that it numbed the English king's pain – and he stayed in his saddle to urge his men on to victory. On and on, the English cavalry and infantry went at the

Scots until eventually the sheer size of the English army began to crush the Scots like an elephant rolling over a mouse.

The Scots were overpowered and Wallace realised it was futile to carry on. Reluctantly, the Scottish leader called a retreat. His brave warriors fled towards the forest to the north, but many of them didn't get away. They were caught by the rampaging, victorious English army.

The Battle of Falkirk ended in disaster for Wallace. For more than 300 days since the Battle of Stirling Bridge, he had kept Scotland free – but now the yoke of slavery was back on the menu. It was time for a change of scene.

15

A new mission

Wallace must have felt bruised, battered and thoroughly miserable after Falkirk. That was a shame, because although he lost the battle, Wallace had actually scored a small victory.

The Battle of Falkirk left Longshanks and his army so hungry and worn out that they didn't have the strength to march all over Scotland and conquer the country properly. So the flame of freedom still flickered, although it was now very faint.

Before long, the English king went back down south, leaving a nest of cronies, stooges and turncoats to keep an eye on Scotland. This encouraged the Scots to fight on against the English in small battles, here and there. Wallace himself even joined in a few of these skirmishes, like the old days before Stirling Bridge.

But Wallace probably couldn't help feeling depressed. He had missed his chance to get rid of the English once and for all at Falkirk. And he must have known the jealous Scottish nobles who thought he should never have been in charge in the first place were happy to see him fail. It seems pretty clear that Wallace was fed up of fighting the English and fed up of being stabbed in the back by other Scots.

Did that mean Wallace gave up his struggle for Scotland's freedom? Never. In fact, Wallace's holiday was actually a new mission.

His plan was to become a Scottish ambassador. In other words, Wallace would put his knowledge of foreign languages to good use by asking powerful people in other countries for help.

So in 1299, Wallace and a handful of loyal knights set sail from Kirkcudbright, on Scotland's south-west coast. Destination – France (and Rome).

First, Wallace planned to try to persuade the French king, Philip IV, to come to the Scots' rescue. Then, he planned to go and ask for help from the pope – the most powerful man in Europe. This all might sound quite straightforward, but actually it was a difficult and dangerous mission.

For a start, just getting to France was hard enough. Wallace had to sail down from Scotland and around the coast of England, across treacherous seas crawling with English warships and other nasty surprises.

It was only a matter of time before Wallace sailed into trouble.

Wallace and his knights had only been at sea for two days when they spotted some unfriendly ships heading their way. As they approached, it became clear that the warlike craft were not English – no such luck. Wallace had run into pirates!

The ships carried the flag of the most feared pirate on the waves – the Red Rover. The Red Rover used to be a French knight called Sir Thomas de Longueville, but after he fell out with the king of France he changed his name and took to the ocean.

For sixteen years, the Red Rover had terrorised all who crossed his path. Now he was master of the seas.

Fearing for their lives, the Scots turned their rudder and set their sails to escape. But the Red Rover's fleet was too fast, and before long the lead pirate ship caught up with them.

The Red Rover leapt aboard Wallace's ship. No sooner had he landed on deck, though, than quick-thinking

Wallace grabbed him. The Red Rover wrestled Wallace but our hero was too strong for him. Soon the pirate begged for mercy.

Wallace took the Red Rover's weapons from him and made the pirate swear on his sword that he would never attack the Scots again. The Red Rover agreed and Wallace spared his life.

For defeating the dastardly pirate, Wallace arrived in France to a hero's welcome. He turned the Red Rover over to the authorities, and the pirate promised to be good from now on.

Then Wallace did something that made the French love him even more. The French were still at war with the English, so Wallace and his men joined the French army for a while to help them out. Wallace defeated the English twice, which impressed King Philip.

But Wallace hadn't really come to win battles for

the French. He wanted Philip to help Scotland. But even though Philip was at war with the English, the French king was worried about upsetting Longshanks too much.

At least Philip did give Wallace a special passport so that he could travel safely across Europe to Rome, to see the pope. Maybe he could help?

16

Under siege

When Wallace got to Rome, he impressed the pope with his story of how the Scots had fought the English empire to defend their little country. The pope especially liked the bit where Wallace told him that the Scots were trying to protect their churches from being destroyed.

After Wallace's visit, the pope warned Longshanks to leave Scotland alone. So did the pope's command make the English king behave? No, it just made Longshanks even angrier. All he cared about now was smashing the Scots and walloping Wallace.

By 1303, Wallace was back in Scotland and Longshanks had launched a new invasion. The English king even offered a reward to any Scot who betrayed Wallace and handed him over to the English. The price on Wallace's head was 300 marks, which was a small fortune in those days. But this reward failed to tempt Wallace's men, who were loyal and honest.

As Longshanks and his army travelled through southern Scotland they burst, battered, burned and blasted everything in their path with swords, clubs, flaming torches and gunpowder.

Eventually, Longshanks reached Dunfermline Abbey,

which was a holy place and the grandest and most beautiful church in Scotland. It was also the place where the English king's sister was buried.

So was Longshanks there to admire the view and perhaps say a prayer or two? Was he there to pay his respects to his sister? And was he worried about how upset the pope would be if he smashed the abbey to smithereens? Of course he wasn't.

Longshanks ordered the abbey to be burned to the ground! But as if that weren't unholy enough, the pope should have seen what Longshanks did next.

Longshanks ordered his son, the prince of Wales, to get his men to climb onto the roof of every Scottish church they came across. This sounds a bit mad, but pay attention.

The men had to strip off the heavy lead sheets that were used to keep the rain off the church roofs and then give the sheets to the English army's blacksmiths. The blacksmiths' task was to melt the lead down and turn it into flaming-hot fireballs for chucking at the Scots. Clever, eh?

In fact, Longshanks used every weapon he could think of against the Scots, as his army continued their rampage around the country. They attacked countless castles, churches, towns and villages. Before long, Longshanks arrived at his ultimate goal – Stirling Castle.

Stirling Castle was the greatest fortress in Scotland, and if it were to fall into Longshanks' clutches it would mean total defeat for the Scots. Longshanks knew this very well. So when he arrived there, the English king began the most awesome castle siege that had ever been seen. The Scots inside Stirling had no chance.

Longshanks' siege weapons were so fierce they would have put even the mighty Roman Empire to shame. Some of them had wooden wheels that were as tall as a man standing on somebody else's shoulders. Others were smaller but just as deadly. They included:

1. Giant darts – the length of two men lying head to toe, these sleek devils were launched by a special catapult. The darts flew up over the castle walls to spear the soldiers inside. Each special catapult was called a ballista. Longshanks had more than a dozen ballistas to fire his deadly darts.

2. Mobile cranes – these could raise a cage of twenty English soldiers high up onto the walls of the castle. Once there, the invaders could open the cage door and jump down into the castle.

3. Steel claws – mounted on the end of a massive pole, each deadly claw was used to pull down the weaker parts of the castle walls, like parapets and overhanging galleries.

4. Tortoises – not real tortoises, but they had a hard metal shell that made them look like a tortoise. Protected under the moving shell, engineers with picks and shovels filled up the moat around the castle with earth and rocks so that the invaders could get close enough to the castle walls to climb them.

5. Giant rats – not real rats, but mighty battering rams that looked like rats. They were as long as a bus and made from wooden beams covered with metal. They were used to break down walls and gates.

6. The War Wolf – this was Longshanks's new secret weapon, the biggest catapult EVER built. But it didn't work very well, which at least gave the Scots a chance.

The Scots in the castle fought bravely to repel the invaders. Once the siege got going, the Scots fired hot tar and boiling oil over the castle walls at their attackers. They dropped hooks down from the castle walls to try to turn the English weapons upside down. But the English were just too many and their weapons too powerful.

Eventually, the Scots began to run out of food and water. On 20 July 1304, those that were left alive finally gave in and surrendered.

When Stirling fell, Scotland's nobles and other leaders believed their nation was finally beaten once and for all. They all surrendered to Longshanks – except for one man.

Now who might that have been?

17

Betrayed

Longshanks offered Scotland's defeated nobles a deal – bring me Wallace and I'll go easy on the rest of you. The Scots agreed, but it was an empty promise. After all that Wallace had done for Scotland, nobody really had the stomach to stab him in the back now. Not even the scheming Scottish nobles.

Even those who did think about betraying Wallace wouldn't have been able to find him, anyway. Wallace and his men had gone back to living off their wits, as a band of outlaws hiding in the hills and woods. To hunt down Wallace, Longshanks was forced to hire a professional army of assassins, spies and turncoats.

One of these was a man called Sir John de Menteith. He had switched sides from Scotland to England and was keen to impress Longshanks. There are a few stories about how Menteith got his hands on Wallace, but one of them begins when Menteith persuaded his nephew to join Wallace's band.

Menteith's nephew told him that Wallace was in Robroyston, just outside Glasgow. One night, Wallace and his men were awoken by somebody hammering at the door.

Straight away, Wallace realised the party of visitors had not come to borrow teabags or collect for charity. It was Menteith and his men.

Once they burst inside, the marauders dragged Wallace's closest companion outside and skewered him on the spot. But Wallace was alert straight away, and as two men tried to grab him he got the better of them. He knocked the brains out of one of them and broke the back of the other on the windowsill. Ouch.

More of Menteith's men rushed in and, eventually, overpowered Wallace. The giant hero was taken out, with his hands and feet tied together.

The turncoats tied Wallace to the saddle of a horse. He was taken on a long journey south to England, where he would face a trial. Wallace spent a night in a dungeon in the town of Carlisle, before a gruelling seventeen-day journey south to London.

According to reports, in London Wallace was paraded through the streets on horseback, with a crown of ivy on his head. The crown was supposed to mock him, like the Romans mocked Jesus before his crucifixion. The crowds that gathered on the streets stood and watched as the fearsome Scottish warrior, who had won great victories against the king of England, passed in front of them.

On 23 August 1305 Wallace was taken to Westminster Hall and tried by judges picked by Longshanks. Wallace was given no right of appeal and the judgement was already decided beforehand. It was a mock trial.

Wallace was convicted of 'treason' against the king of England. But Wallace pointed out that it was impossible for him to commit treason against Longshanks. 'The king of England is not my king,' he roared.

Yet the judgement had been passed – Wallace was condemned to die a horrible, grisly, blood-spattered death.

18

The ultimate price

After the judgement was passed, Wallace was taken outside the hall and stripped naked. Then the brave hero was shackled to a hurdle, which was a device used to drag him along the ground on his back. The hurdle was attached to the tails of two horses.

For four hours, in the sweltering conditions of a hot summer's day, Wallace was dragged through the streets of London. People threw rubbish, rotten food and stones at him as he bumped and scraped along the cobbles. Others struck him with cudgels and whips. His pain must have been agonising.

Eventually, Wallace arrived at a place called Smithfield – the place of execution. The naked prisoner was unshackled and shaken to his feet. With his hands tied behind him, Wallace was forced to climb the ladder to a high scaffold, where he would be hanged.

From the dizzying heights of the scaffold, Wallace could see the huge crowd that had gathered to watch him die. The bloodthirsty mob was about to be greatly entertained by the execution of the Scottish patriot, because Wallace was to be killed three times over. He was first to be hanged, then drawn and finally quartered.

It was a horrible way to go. Even reading about it is enough to make your blood run cold and the hairs on the back of your neck bristle. Just imagine it.

First, the hanging. Wallace's head was placed in the hangman's noose. As the rope tightened around his neck, Wallace was strangled until nearly dead.

Then, the drawing. Wallace was revived after his encounter with the hangman's noose by a bucket of cold water, thrown over his head. This was done to make sure he could feel the next bit of agonising pain. A deep cut was then made in his belly and Wallace's intestines were drawn out slowly like a long string of sausages.

In front of Wallace was a bonfire. The long sausage-string of his guts was thrown into the bonfire and burned. Then Wallace's heart was plucked out while it was still beating and shown to the mob, who cheered. After that, Wallace's head was cut off and held up for all to see, and the mob cheered even louder.

Finally, the quartering. A big, shiny meat cleaver was brandished by the executioner. He used it like a butcher, to chop Wallace's body into four parts, each with an arm or leg still attached.

Just in case you were in any doubt, poor Wallace was well and truly dead by now! His head was stuck on a spike on London Bridge, where his grisly features looked out over the city until his skull was pecked clean by gulls and crows. Well, at least they had good taste.

So what happened to the other bits of Wallace's body?

His right arm was taken to Newcastle, in northern England, and was hung above the town's smelly sewers.

The rest of Wallace's body was taken to Scotland. His left arm was hung up at Stirling. His right leg was put up at Berwick and his left leg at Perth.

This was a WARNING to anybody else in Scotland who had ideas about trying to end the tyranny of Longshanks. Wallace had battled to save Scotland from slavery and paid the ultimate price. And Scotland was still under Longshanks' iron fist.

But does all this mean Wallace had sacrificed his life for nothing? Certainly not! In fact, Wallace's story doesn't end here at all. His life inspired others to begin a long quest to free his country . . .

Epilogue

Wallace's heroic life and brave death made the Scots realise it was possible to stand up for themselves. They didn't have to be slaves if they really didn't want to.

Wallace had died because his people didn't stick together and he was betrayed. But now the Scots understood that if they DID stick together to help each other, they could get their country back and be rid of their conquerors forever.

The Scots figured out that what they needed was a strong king who had Wallace's courage and skill as a warrior, as well as some special gifts that only a king can possess.

So just a few months after Wallace was executed, a new monarch stepped forward to restart the struggle for Scotland's freedom. His name was Robert the Bruce.

Bruce was a member of one of Scotland's most powerful noble families, and he was inspired by Wallace's bravery and patriotism. In fact, it was probably young Bruce who knighted Wallace after Wallace's victory at the Battle of Stirling Bridge all those years ago.

There isn't enough room in this book to squeeze in

Bruce's brilliant adventures. But if you want to find out how Bruce beat the English army and made Wallace's dreams come true . . . hunt down a copy of *Robert The Bruce And All That*!

But this story has not really been about Scotland beating England, or England beating Scotland. It's about much more than that.

Thanks to Wallace, the Scots and the English eventually learned to live side by side as good friends – because Wallace showed that one group of people should never try to make slaves of another.

In fact, thanks to heroes like Wallace, people all over the world are inspired to stand up for anyone who is bullied or treated unfairly.

In Scotland, Wallace's memory lives on in the new national parliament in Edinburgh. It's a place where every

Scot has a say in how the country is run. The Scots decided to build the parliament in 1997 – exactly 700 years after Wallace's great victory at the Battle of Stirling Bridge.

And Wallace doesn't just live on in Edinburgh, but all over Scotland – in his statues, monuments and paintings. As we have also discovered, there are legendary Wallace caves, Wallace stones and Wallace forests scattered all around.

Open up a good map, and it should reveal which Wallace treasures might be lurking near your or your relatives' and friends' homes. If you visit these places and bring your imagination, you'll find Wallace's world is still all around you.